9 Day Energy Reset

The rituals presented in this guide are not a replacement for professional medical, legal, psychological, marital, or financial advice. You possess free will and you are ultimately responsible for the quality of your life. The author and affiliated organizations are not responsible for your decisions, choices or actions.

Copyright © 2016 by Mona Van Joseph

October 31, 2016

Thoughtful & professional editing by Gail at
www.customcrosswords.com

www.9DayER.com

"Be profoundly grateful for where you are, right now. Consider that you have exactly the perfect foundation to create precisely what you want; from here, from this space. Pragmatically look around you and celebrate what supports your vision, and reject, without hesitation, what does not."   *Mona Van Joseph*

9 Day Energy Reset

There is a reason you are reading these words.

Maybe this guide came to you because you want to create something different, or you are celebrating a personal milestone. Perhaps you have had the loss of a treasured person or job, or are experiencing financial upheaval. You may have received this guide as a gift because someone wishes the absolute best for you. Maybe you realize that you are ready to be engaged in a new learning or spiritual adventure and want a fuller, purposeful, and more satisfying life.

Or, maybe this came to you because you feel stuck.

The information in this guide will help. Unlike other information on the subject of manifestation, the specific rituals outlined here will keep you focused on your goal. This 9 day energy reset ritual will allow you to align with your highest potential. By focusing your energy and awareness, you will discover that you have complete control over what you draw to you. You will find that, by channeling the right energy and being aware that you have created everything (so far) in this lifetime, you can begin to mold your future toward what you desire. You can manifest a more fulfilling life.

For 9 days, avoid discussing this specific ritual with anyone. The more you keep this ritual to yourself, the more powerful it will be. The reason for this secrecy is that people, as well-intentioned as they appear to be, will tend to undermine your progress. The exception being those in a committed relationship/friendship may do the ritual together and discuss/celebrate the signs of progress along the way.

This is designed to be a simple and immediate way for you to relax into the energy that creates your most empowered life. While engaging in this specific ritual, read the words of the marvelous spiritual leaders, past and present, and be inspired. The ritual works because you will make your desires an expected priority. This is a fast-track way of aligning your entire being with the most productive energy available to you. You are receiving the energy you seek to draw to you and staying aware of how it is manifesting.

Rituals give us a meaningful way to *do* something besides *just* being positive. They help to create the foundation for a better mindset. What you think about defines who you are, and the actions you engage in from this moment forward will define who you are to become. When these two things are brought into harmony, you will realize your power and potential. Nothing happens until you take action. You are now ready to live a more meaningful and enriched life. Now is the time for memorable experiences, loving relationships, and the creation of your most ideal life. You are the center of your own Universe.

The best way to predict your future is to design it with your awareness and focus.

Clearing

Before you begin this ritual, you must first clear space for that new energy and the new you. Clearing your physical environment helps you to clear your mind. As you clear your living space and those unnecessary items from your past, it will allow you to reconcile emotions from that issue or circumstance. You want something new or different, and you want to move forward. Clearing is the first step toward having what you want. It may take you a day, or a week, or a month, but this task has to be done first to help you change your energy.

Look around your home. What it looks like right now directly reflects how you feel about yourself and what's going on in your mind. Do the public areas of your home (living room, kitchen, bathroom) look tidy and well-kept? If those areas are organized and tidy, is your bedroom and private rooms a complete catch-all (or disaster area) for everything else? Does your guest room/garage store all that other stuff? Do you rent a storage space for all the things that don't fit into your living space?

Think about it... you are all fabulously put together when you leave your home (your public face), but your home isn't entirely organized. Your living environment is a direct representation of your inner environment. Though you have the best intentions of creating the life you really desire, you are not really prepared to live that new or better life. You have created no space for that new experience or thing to live. You may miss what is specifically meant for you because you are not clear, open, and ready to receive. Too much clutter in your environment probably means too much clutter in your mind and spirit.

Before beginning the 9 Day Energy Reset, the landscape of your physical living space and your mind, must be cleared of the overgrowth. You must prune away what has taken over your personal space, and pull the weeds of the past to create an open environment for something new. This needs to be done so you are not distracted from the pure focus of creating your most authentic life.

The exercises that follow will focus on clearing away the things in your physical or mental space that consciously, or unconsciously, hold you back. You will clear away anything that represents aspects of the "old" you that you wish to change. You will remove anything that causes you pain, guilt, sorrow, heartache, or loss. These are emotions that are holding you away from the life you deserve to live.

This Universe was created for you ... and you are created for the Universe. You are an important contribution to this world. The most essential responsibility as a creation in this world is to be true to, and live up to, your utmost potential. The quality of your life IS your responsibility, and you can manifest anything you wish to bring into your life. From this moment forward, there is no one to blame, no one to curse, and no one holding you back from what you want. Every human accomplishment begins as a thought first, and you will be creating the thoughts that lead you to a more fulfilled life. It's very simple; you just have to WANT something…and then be aware when the Universe is giving it to you. It's okay to want what YOU want! When you make peace with this concept, you can create it into your life.

Your spirit has been given the gift of a body and a mind. The only thing you truly own is what is developed within that initial gift: education, experiences, feelings, adventures, and love. All pleasures are based out of *those* possessions. When our physical possessions possess us, they are no longer enjoyable. So if anything has become too much trouble to keep, let it go. Look for what feeds and contributes to what you can really own, and stop holding on to anything if it does not represent *you* living the most loving and productive life.

Step One: Purge and Clean Your Living Space

Before you can get to the real work of creating and manifesting, you must let go of everything that represents anything negative in your living space. Your personal space will best serve you if it is purged of clutter, and all the horizontal surfaces (countertops, dressers, desks) become clear landscapes.

Remove any plants that are not healthy and thriving.

Remove pictures of negative people, or anyone that has hurt you in any way, so those pictures are not in your line of vision.

This is the time to get rid of clothing that you have not worn in over a year, and donate those items to a charitable organization. Remove everything in your closet, and only return to it what you've worn in the last six months. Then, be really discerning. Does it really look that great on you? How many pairs of black shoes do you really need? Most people can purge half of what is in their closet and not miss it. Think of the people that could really use that coat (that you wore once, three years ago) this winter. You will generate good will, and will recognize the power you have in true releasing.

It is time to critically evaluate the kitchen. How many duplicate items do you have? Did you use the pasta maker in the last 3 years? Get rid of whatever you are not actively using.

Once you have cleaned the interior of your home, tackle the garage and outdoor landscaping, if applicable, and make sure those areas are free of clutter and weeds.

Clean out any area that has become a catch-all for anything, including your car.

Give away or donate what you are not using. Throw away anything chipped or broken. If you need any of these items in the future, those items will find their way to you.

Step Two: Purge and Clean Your Mind Space

After your living space has been cleared, now is the time to dump the negativity that is taking up valuable manifestation space in your mind. You cannot control anything from the past, so it is time to let all painful emotions and grudges go. Take all the time you need to do the exercise below, and allow yourself to relive the emotions so you can completely release them.

You must feel the pain before you can heal the pain. With one sheet of paper and a pencil, write down grudges, guilt, painful relationships, nasty co-workers, grief, and any event that has caused you anger, sadness, regret, or sorrow. Write down any issues where you may have wronged someone, and in the same flow of thought, write them an apology. If a specific person stands out, and those emotions feel especially unresolved, write them a letter (as described below). This is free-flow, emotional, vomit-writing, with absolutely no limits. Every stinking thought that you have allowed unlimited roaming privileges in your mind goes on the paper. Fill up all the space on one side of the paper and cram as much of this dirty mental laundry as possible on the page.

When you use a pencil in this exercise, you will hear yourself write the words on the paper. Most young students used pencils when first learning, so this specific exercise will touch an intimate part of your memory. When you cannot think of anything else to write, end this exercise by writing the following words on the back of the sheet of paper:

"*I release these past events for my new beginning.*"

Write a letter to someone you dearly loved that has passed over. Feel all the emotions associated with that person. Tell them what you always wanted to tell them in this letter. Express why you loved them and what they taught you. Write about the best things about the two of you, and why you knew that he or she was placed in your life. End this exercise with the following words at the bottom of the letter:

"*The great love of this relationship guides me through my day and leads me to new loves.*"

If there is a past relationship (partner, spouse, parent, sibling, work associate) for whom you hold great pain or need closure with, write them a letter. In that letter, tell them everything that upset you about the relationship. The more details you write in this letter, the more productive this exercise will be. This letter is not to be mailed or given to the person. In the closing paragraph of the letter, write why you think this relationship was important to you and why you are stronger (or more learned) as a result. When you cannot think of anything else to write, end this exercise with the following words:

"*I release this past relationship to embrace the ones I deserve.*"

This last exercise is forgiveness of self. On a sheet of paper, write down all the things that you regret, feel guilty about, and/or didn't do to the best of your ability. Everything and anything that you have ever beaten yourself up about goes on this sheet of paper. Write about your role in things that didn't go well. Write about any shame or misplaced anger. Write about that person you didn't treat well who didn't deserve it. Confess everything, so you allow yourself to remove the last sticky thorns of self-sabotage. When you have exhausted the list, end this exercise with the following words:

"I forgive myself to allow my most authentic and loving self to be revealed."

Under the phrase of each of these exercises, sign the paper with your official legal signature. Then, crumple them up and safely burn them. Drink a cup of hot tea or water while the paper is burning, so it will allow you to feel warmth in your chest as you release these thoughts from your personal energy.

Moving forward, if one of these ugly thoughts creeps back into your mind, or anger or sadness creeps in, grab a sticky note pad, tear off a sheet and, on the sticky side, write that painful or negative thought. Seal it together, and on the outside of the folded note write the words, "I release." When you get home at the end of your day, safely burn the sticky note.

Once you have cleaned and purged your living and mind space, you are ready for the Home Energy Reset Ritual.

Your Priorities

There are six steps to getting what you want. Getting what you want is not necessarily about "affirmations" or "thinking positive." It's about the energy of what you want. This Universe is designed for you to live the most productive and soul-inspired live. When your intent is to live in this fashion, you become more aware of the gifts that care constantly presented to you.

Step 1 - *Be grateful for where you are right now*.

This gratitude may arrive from a place of pain, or joy. It doesn't matter how the moment arrives for this exact perspective because it has been given to you as a gift. List all the things that are happening, without thought of the "good" or 'bad" of your situation. List all the people that support you. List what is actually working for you and stop beaming energy toward what is not.

Step 2 – *Do not complain about your situation.*

This is energy. You are the only one who can draw the energy to you to change anything about your life. With any great loss, there will be a mourning period. Honor that period by surrounding yourself with the people and situations that will help to heal that pain. At some point, you will be ready to move forward; when you are ready, you will stop complaining. You can acknowledge the sadness, or the anger without dwelling in it.

Step 3 – *Know WHAT you want.*

The Universe cannot draw to you what you want unless you know what you want. What you think about is drawn to you. Instead of thinking about what you don't want, concentrate instead on what you do want. Flip around any thought of pain to the opposite, and into a goal. For example: "I'll never find someone to love." to "I want the perfect companion-of-choice in my life." OR, "I always struggle with money." to "I want to never have to worry about money."

Step 4 – *Prepare for what you want.*

Start preparing your environment as though what you want is about to happen. If you want a loving companion, make space in your home as though that person will be arriving. Present yourself as though you could meet that person any day, or any time. If you want more money, look for a job that is more enjoyable and pays you more. Decide to write that book. Turn a hobby into extra income. Most importantly, clear away any reminder of what you do not want represented in your life. If there's an ex-partner, stow away those pictures and memories. If you're wasting money, find creative ways to save more and make more. Sell or give away what you are not using. Empty space will be filled with new and more satisfying people, adventures and opportunities.

Step 5 – Be AWARE

Be aware, because things will begin to happen quickly. Invitations, opportunities and recognition are all a part of awareness. That man or woman that catches your eye at the coffee shop, an invitation to a gathering, or opportunity to learn something new crosses your radar. What you want will require that you get a little out of your usual routine. Allow that to happen. New environments will allow you to talk about what you want. Without guile or guilt, you can boldly make statements like, "I am seeking my companion-of-choice," or "I'm looking for a new career adventure."

Step 6 – Be YOU

Be you in every situation. Believe that everything around you accepts you for who you are. The more authentic you allow yourself to be, the more of what you truly want will be drawn to you.

Ritual for Home Energy Reset
Items:

You'll need a large sage burning stick or incense

Spray bottle; a new one, specifically for this task, with no printed words on it

Gallon bottle of distilled water

Permanent marker

This ritual is performed after your living space is cleaned.

At least 24 hours before performing this ritual, use the permanent marker to write the word "LOVE" on the outside of the distilled water jug, and on the outside of the spray bottle. After 24 hours, fill the spray bottle with the distilled water.

Close all the doors and windows of your home. Light the sage burning wand or incense stick. Let the flame catch on the end of the stick, and then blow it out so the embers at the end are "smoking." Carry the smoking sage wand or incense stick in your right hand. Face the inside of your front door, and extend your right arm toward the top center of the doorframe.

Step about three feet back from the interior of your front door, and draw an imaginary, counter-clockwise circle with the smoking sage around the inside frame of the front door. Then, turn to your left and walk the entire perimeter of the inside of your house, counter-clockwise, almost touching the walls with the smoking stick. If you have more than one floor, smoke the downstairs first (or whichever floor your front door is on), and then the upstairs, and then the basement or lowest floor... and remember the garage.

Go back to the front door and make a clockwise circle (as described above) around the inside frame of the door. Turn to your right and walk clockwise with the smoking sage around the entire inside perimeter of your house.

After the counterclockwise and clockwise circle of your home, you'll be back at the inside of your front door. Make one more clockwise circle around the inside frame of your front door.

Go outside and face your front door. Circle the outside frame of the door clockwise, and do one clockwise circle around the outside perimeter of your house, if possible. If you are in an apartment or attached house, you do not need to sage around the entire building.

Extinguish the sage stick in a small amount of the distilled water and discard.

Open ALL the windows in the home and turn on any fans. Allow the house to "air" for about 5 minutes. Take your "Love" spray bottle and lightly spray toward the corners of the inside of your home.

Close all the windows and drink a glass of water from the gallon jug with the word "Love" on it. Give all the plants in your home 1/2 cup of the water from this jug. Share this water with any person or pet that lives with you.

You ARE Love

You are a creation of love. The entire environment in which you live is designed specifically for you to be in this world. Think about everything that had to be just right for you to be here. Your specific parents with their specific genes, and their love, made your physical being. At the moment you were conceived, everything needed to be perfect for you to be here. It does not matter HOW you got here, or even how you were raised. The important thing is you are here now, and you can begin to create the life you want now.

It is important for you to recognize that you are always supported by this love. Even though you may feel troubled or challenged, or want something different, the fundamental truth is you are made of love. What you love, and what you think about, is constantly attracted to you. When you relax into this love and allow it to flow through you, you can have the life that you want. The reverse is also true. If something is causing you pain, the love of the Universe will remove it from your life. Realize and agree that this environment is always allowing you to grow into your potential and happiness.

Everything changes when you apply discipline to what you allow your mind to absorb. The most powerful decision a person can make is to change and control his or her mind. What directs your mind is your spirit — the essence of who you really are. Once you allow the most infinite aspect of your being to have control over the quality of your life, you take the first step to drawing to you a more meaningful existence.

Most people do not know how to accept this grand love. They constantly push, or do, or give, and wonder why it is never "their turn." It is always "your turn" when you open yourself to receiving this grand love instead of saying "no" to it.

How many times have you told someone who wants to help you, "No, thank you, I can do this myself." Or, "I don't need help, I'm good." Or complained, "Nothing good ever happens for me?" Or, "Nobody ever gives me anything." All of these statements push love away. Love is constantly surrounding you, and will agree with whatever energy you present.

For you to have what you want in this life, it's time for you to say "yes," and accept everything that is being offered to you. It's incredibly powerful to learn to receive in direct balance to what you give. The 9 Day Energy Reset is based on 80% receiving and 20% giving. It is set up this way for you to concentrate more on what the Universe is presenting to you, rather than what you have to offer. What you have to offer is valuable, and you will not spend any time proving to anyone your value during the ritual of your choice. With that thought, and during these rituals, do not volunteer your help, or resources, to those people who assume it. Wait until you are asked. And then, if you are asked, you can decide pragmatically if the volunteering or assisting will be of value to you in some way. Remember, anything that teaches you something, or could be beneficial to you toward your goal, is worth your energy to volunteer or participate. Anything that you resent doing, or depletes your reserves or sense of well-being, is a "no."

Below are some of the most powerful and truthful ways to decline those assumptive invitations or requests:

• For people that assume you will volunteer:
"Thank you for asking, and as much as I would like to help, I have a personal project that I am committed to complete at that time." It is none of anyone's business what your project is, but if they push, emphasize that it is personal.

• For people who ask you for money:
"I am fully invested right now and unable to loan/give you the money you are requesting. However, I think you are smart enough and resourceful enough to figure this out and I am looking forward to hearing how you solve this." You are not an ATM for someone else's irresponsibility or emergency.

• An invitation to an event where you are expected to volunteer, cook, donate or contribute:
"That won't work for me right now, I have another commitment."

• Someone who dumps their work you (and typically takes credit for your work, and is not your boss or direct supervisor):

"I know that I have assisted you in the past with this project, but I am committed to my boss for one of her priorities right now, so if you want me to help you again on the task, you'll need to clear it with her." They typically will not ask your boss if you can do their work for them, because your boss will realize that if you've been doing that person's work, why does he or she need to keep that person employed?

• Someone who gossips:
Immediately interrupt them and say, "My apologies, I just remembered something I need to do right now." The last thing you need during your Energy Reset is someone that perpetuates any negative energy.

There is a certain control in being a "giver," but ultimately you may become resentful if you are not being receptive as well. Sometimes a person gives specifically because he or she wants control over a situation. A person might usually treat to dinner or an activity, because they know that if they organize the meal or event, it will typically be the experience they expect. They are "giving" for things to go a certain way. Doing this giving in joy and love, with no expectation of a return favor, is authentic sharing. However, if it is done to impress, or to count on something in return, then it is conditional. Conditional giving is not really true giving.

No giving or kindness is ever wasted. It may not appear as though you get something back, but you do. You get the gift of knowing that the money you just donated will help someone else. You get the gift of knowing that helping a person through a rough patch has put them back on track. And, you get to remember that because of you, a dear friend found the perfect job or opportunity. Most importantly, you get the gift of people acknowledging you for your most loving self.

The 9 Day Energy Reset requires you to be open to receive, and in some cases be a little uncomfortable with a different way of attracting to you what you want. This world is a co-operative, co-dependent one. Great love is always in action in your life. Make the decision to be still and open, and allow yourself to accept everything as a special gift, opportunity, or lesson. Receptiveness, allowing others to help, allowing yourself to hear the message, and participating in life, is the key to having what you want. This is about your magnetic and receptive energy, not your dynamic and giving energy.

Think of this as though the world is a big savings bank. You've been giving and giving and you have, up until now, been saying "no" to what is trying to come back to you. Now is the time to say "yes" to invitations, favors, meals, coffee visits, gestures of goodwill, and lessons. Now is the time to break the habit of doing everything yourself. Let people give what they are willing and able to give to you, and accept with gratitude what they offer.

Relative to what you wish to draw into your life, if there are people that "owe" you anything, now is the time to call in those favors. Each of these people you contact will be people that you have helped in some way. Remember how incredibly grateful he or she was to you when you were there to help? Keep in mind that when you reach out, it is likely that they *want* to do something to thank you. Ask that person to assist you in the specific way you know he or she can. Ask that person for the money they owe you. Ask that person to introduce you to one of their colleagues, or if their company is hiring, the manager of a certain department. Ask that person for a favor. Just ask. If it turns out that they are unwilling or unable to assist you, then it is time to let that relationship fade into the past with gratitude and love.

Lastly, and most importantly, there is no such thing as a curse on you, or that you have "bad energy." If you seem to attract uncomfortable situations, it is because that specific lesson is one you need to learn from. Once you learn from any situation, you can release the energies associated. If they seem to repeat, it means you have not yet learned from it. The more painful they are when they repeat, the more important they are to resolve.

Do not believe anyone that tells you that you have bad energy, or a hole in your karma, or that they are the only person who can shift that, or solve that problem for you. That is a con. It is always a con. You also do not need to sign up for any subscription service claiming miraculous results, because you can do this yourself. Once you adopt the energies presented here toward your most empowered life, then you will ultimately see that you really do have the power.

The way to have the life you want is through energy and awareness — casting out the energy of what you want, and being actively aware of what is presented to you as a result. You take the step, and make the shift, by accepting what is presented, and loving yourself enough to dare to receive what you want.

Love is all you need.

9 Day Energy Reset

Prior to starting, take care of anything you have been postponing, so there are no excuses with finishing all 9 days of this ritual. You've already purged and cleaned your living space, and already addressed the issues clouding your mind. You've already completed the Home Cleansing Ritual and have created the environment for things to shift and change.

Take care of any doctor appointments you've been putting off. Receive the okay from your doctor for moderate physical exercise. Take care of any maintenance with your car or home. Wash and fill up your car. You want your life to be at its usual "normal" starting point at the beginning of this ritual so you may recognize the subtle (and maybe not so subtle) changes that will occur.

The 9 Day Energy Reset is about the expectation of change, and being receptive. It is effective when you feel stuck, stagnant, or don't know what to do. It is 9 days of energy, discipline, and awareness. It is about receiving inspiration, information, signs, coincidences, energy, and love. It's about getting a little out of your comfort zone, and into learning and experiencing new things. You may do some modest "giving" gestures, but they are by your decision and in your control. You are also breaking the habit of thinking negatively, or doing anything that works against you. You are no longer making excuses, or treating anyone else as though they are more important than you.

You may wish to do this ritual when you know there is a project that requires your undivided attention to complete. Perhaps you are finally going to finish that book or screenplay during these 9 days. Or, maybe you challenge yourself to do something new each day of the ritual. Though it is preferred to clear/purge your living space prior to the start of this ritual, some people tidy up a bit before starting, and use the 9 days to do the major letting go of what's been collected over the years. Though you may begin this ritual on any day, the best day to start is on the 1st, 10th, or 19th day of the month. When you begin on these days, you are aligning with the numerical vibration of that day of the month to coincide with your energy reset.

Day 1 focus (the 1st, 10th, or 19th of the month) = SELF

You have made the decision to make yourself a priority. Consider the things you can do to better yourself in any way and prepare yourself for your upcoming success.

This is the divine agreement between you and your higher self. Your spirit chose this moment in time to exist. You chose what your body looks like; as well as your family, significant loves; how smart you are; and the meaningful relationships you attract in this lifetime. Your spirit chose to manifest for a specific purpose and your quest in this lifetime is to achieve your highest potential. Take care of your mind, your body and your spiritual alignment.

You chose all the people that presented significant challenges and it is always about learning claiming the importance of this moment. Learn and then release. Be especially attentive to people who have nothing to gain regarding your issue. The older you are, the more you have accomplished even though it may not seem that way. You are exactly the person you are for the purpose of this lifetime.

This is also the balance of the masculine and the feminine within you. If you find that those scales are imbalanced, it's time to make the appropriate adjustments. If you've been constantly questing after a goal, consider shifting your perspective to one of patience and waiting. Or, you might want to become more dynamic if you have been thinking that the goal will arrive with little effort on your part.

Day 2 focus (the 2nd, 11th, or 20th of the month) = PARTNERSHIPS

Acknowledge and be grateful for the partnerships/friendships that have supported you. This is the day to realize who is in your support system.

It is now time on your part to acknowledge the credibility of friendships without the conscious knowledge of the people considered. This is where you extend a favor or two behind the scenes on their behalf. You will find that by touting someone else's business, friendship, or good experience that more beneficial tidings find their way to you. This is a way to add more depth to your business, relationships or situations simply by recognizing greatness in others. Sing the praises of someone you care about.

Our best friends and most meaningful relationships reflect what we like about ourselves. By touting the wonderful things about others, you are actually talking about the things within you that you admire. The flip side of this exercise is true as well; if we do not appreciate something about another person, than we are considering aspects of our more negative nature.

Envy is the most destructive characteristic we can adopt. What it tells us about ourselves is that we cannot tolerate someone having something we desire for ourselves and maybe we think they do not deserve such success. The shifted perspective claims that the person who has triggered envy within us might be distinguished for what they have accomplished. The person goes from being criticized to being celebrated.

The most disarming way to deal with envy is to imagine that anything another can do we can do for ourselves. We all have something within us that is unique. It is up to us to embrace what we can contribute that brings us abundance and contentment. By complimenting the accomplishments of others you actually bring yourself greater approving energy by those around you.

Your atmosphere becomes one of thoughtful genuineness.

Day 3 focus (the 3rd, 12th, or 21st day of the month) = GOALS

What do you want to draw into your life? What would you like to change?

Tell everyone that has the potential to help you about your intentions. If you are seeking a loving companion, a new job, a vacation, or a material thing, this is the time to talk about your objective. Do not be shy; this is about you expanding your circle to bring you what you know in your heart you may have. Contact people from the past, communicate your goals and then allow those goals to materialize. Write down what you want, place it in an envelope, seal it and put it on your refrigerator with a magnet.

Form a clear picture of what you want and talk about it.

Allowing yourself permission to create what you want is the way to bring forth a fulfilling life. You will eventually teach others the way to fashion their own goals and desires. By the experience of manifesting your desires, you can easily set an example of how to work with the flow of all things. There are no accidents and pure intent on your part allows the Universe to direct to you exactly what you require.

If you are emphasizing lack in your life then that is what you will receive, if you do not think there's enough, then that is what you will experience. Operate from the perspective of abundance and that will bring observable and measurable results. You will find that the person or thing will find its way to you with very little effort on your part. Your poise will be one of awareness and then the energy to take action when the appropriate omen occurs.

Clear intention allows you flexibility and the ability to adapt to rapid changes. The more disruptive the flow of events, the more your current perspective or environment was not working toward your best possible potential. Embrace that this discomfort is actually moving you toward your right of abundance.

Pure intent produces beneficial results.

Day 4 focus (the 4th, 13th, or 22nd day of the month) = FOUNDATION

Concentration of what allows you to feel secure and at the same time liberates you.

Check that every financial, material, and physical item is working in accord to your question. This is about the tedious task of checking all the details. Make sure the financing, people, and materials required for the question are available. This is about selfishly making sure that all aspects of the project are working on your behalf. This is not a good time for assumption of capacity and ability. You are personally required to perform this "checking" as it will truly affect you.

You must first care for yourself before you can care for anything else.

Defining what is important to you is the first step in creating an authentic sense of self. This is about living up to your own potential and expectations. It is actually easier to live up to another's idea of success and accomplishment because you do not have to decide for yourself what's important. We have been cultured that selfishness is distasteful but it is those with a strong sense of self that have accomplished the greatest things in their lifetime. They are not trying to live up to their Mother or Father's expectations – they are living up to their own. That is a much more difficult concept to initially grasp because it means that you will probably have to change your "foundation" or support system in some way.

Your perspective and potential are unique to you and therefore, are the individual expression of the Divine within you. Trust that you know the right thing to do and you will know how to handle any challenge or opportunity that arises. You are no good to yourself or anyone else if you have not decided how you will live your life from this point forward.

Your recognition of your own self worth and creating your most nurturing foundation will liberate you.

Day 5 focus (the 5th, 14th, or the 23rd day of the month) = COMMUNICATION

Listen for the messages that seem to speak directly to you. The messages can come from a co-worker, a friend, a song on the radio, a newscast, movie, or TV show.

Consider this a checkpoint for your progress. See what emotions are mirrored back to you today. This is the time of checking how others respond to you and your goals. Act on those encouraging words and meditate on what you resist hearing. Remember, everyone in your circle is here to assist you in becoming the most empowered being that you can conceive yourself to be. There is no loss of power; you are reserving action for the correct moment.

All doubts about this next step must be answered before you will know if this is the right move to make. If you are deciding about a new career opportunity, make sure you know all about the company you are considering. If you have asked about a relationship, there are still unanswered concerns. This is a time of inquiry not action. Form the most enlightening questions and then inquire. Take the time to consider your life path.

You are amazingly powerful and others are recognizing your strength. This is a time in your life where opportunities are presenting themselves more quickly because you have established your potential for a meaningful partnership; career advancement; or beginning any project on your own. Keep your resources close to chest and be patient at this time.   Be cheerful and optimistic that the appropriate information will unfold at the exact moment for you to make this decision.   You are mature enough spiritually to handle the situation presented to you, but (on a soul level) you are not willing to sacrifice the time if the decision does not serve your highest potential.

You are at a point in your life where (your) time is your most important commodity; nothing should waste this precious gift.   Anything you choose to bestow your attention needs to be of appropriate value.   This question is about preparing your turning point in this life.   You are on the brink of desired changes; make sure that you are serving your best interest.

Day 6 focus (the 6th, 15th, and 24th day of the month) = LOVE RELATIONSHIPS

Concentrate on what and who brings you joy. Do what you love and be with the people you love.

This is about true love, deep meaningful friendships, and the liberation that accompanies this level of companionship with another. Specifically, this is about celebrating or attracting those people who accept and love you for exactly who you are. And, if you already have that one special "companion of choice" in your life, it is time to rejoice that you of you are creating something greater than you could have ever accomplished on your own. If you are seeking to incorporate great love in your life, then now is the time that the Universe is blessing you with the tools to do so.

I am now willing to experience blissful love in my life. Surrendering our guard to great love is the most difficult barrier to dissolve. You will know the right person when he or she empowers you to feel greater than yourself. The most remarkable aspect of this attraction is that you want the same for them. You love this person enough so you both continue to learn and grow. The correct relationships allow us to feel authentic and liberated.

We choose at a soul level that which will bring us the great joyful lessons in this lifetime with another being. When we find each other, there is no stress about how to behave, our outward appearance, or the level of material wealth. It is uncalculated and something beyond the rules of the world.

Day 7 focus (the 7th, 16th, and 25th day of the month) = SPIRITUAL ALIGNMENT

Recognize and be grateful for the energy working for you.

What is your spiritual foundation? Deciding what motivates you spiritually is the key to living your most authentic life. You may decide to return to the spiritual roots of your upbringing. Or you may simply decide that you will live your life guided by love, compassion and purpose. Define how the power of the Universe will work through you and decide where to place your faith. Place faith in yourself first, and then faith that the Universe always supports your vision.

You may begin to recognize how your unique awareness has a specific place in on this Earth, and that will help to guide you.

This is the point when experiences in life bring you more joy. It is a time of trusting that you deserve the gifts that are currently presented. Gifts such as love, devotion, faith, opportunities, pleasure and abundance are now aspects of your reality. This trusting power allows you to believe in the splendor of life again. It is a knowing that divine timing is now working with you to reward you for all the work, energy and love you have given.

You are becoming more aware of your power and potential by keeping your heart open.

Day 8 focus (the 8th, 17th, and 26th day of the month) = DESTINY

Recognizing what you love to do, how it can contribute to the world, and how you can do more of that.

You are about to enjoy the swing of circumstances in your favor and it is timely to prepare for that change. Study every communication coming toward you now with the perspective of preparing for action. One of the items you receive will grant you clear indication of timing. In your divine state, you have chosen this moment.

This time represents great potential when your energies and the energies around you have formed critical mass. Something magnificent is about to be born and your mundane human self cannot rush the process. Simply allow this opportunity to unfold with the patient expectancy of something superb. Be confident that all your challenges and clear focus are about to be rewarded.

Consider how your environment must change to accommodate your new way of life and prepare for that change as you wait. You won't have time to attend to all the small things once your door opens for you. Connect with all of the people who have supported you through all of your challenges and let them know you are expecting something big any moment. Enjoy the anticipation of something great developing for you.

Watch the Universe unfold for you.

Day 9 focus (the 9th, 18th, or 27th day of the month) = COMPLETION

What can you finish today?

The work is joyful, the events memorable, and the people involved are working with clear heart and focus. Your hard work and single-mindedness now allow you success, prosperity, abundance, and most of all the understanding of the significance of love. This is the realization of your potential, the understanding of your place in this world and the assurances that your life will never be the same. All that you seek to have in your life is at your fingertips now.

This moment is the realization of why you were born into this lifetime. It is the identification of your purpose, the understanding of the power of love, and the result of living your life to its highest potential. The external around you is reflecting what your mind has embraced. This is the most powerful and fortunate combination of all the combination.

Celebrate all of those individuals who showed you the Universe was moving through them to help you; even those people who made you upset or appeared to be working against you. All the aspects that occurred to bring you to this place had to be there for you to succeed and realize this moment. Allow yourself to appreciate just how much you are loved because you chose to love everything about your life.

This cycle places you in a position to assist someone else and in doing so you help him or her realize his or her chosen destiny. Since you now understand that you had to recognize and act upon your unique gift first before you could be any assistance to someone else, the power behind your gift of assistance is now genuine. By your achievement through what you love, you can now recognize the true potential of another.

You have earned this pinnacle, now, what is the next one?

By doing this exercise, you are agreeing to receive more, and refrain from mindless giving. You are in a reserving and magnetic energy, and you are happily patient. Focus on what you want and do the tasks and training that may be required. During these 9 days, be open to anything that seems to be meant for you to see, hear, or experience. Pay attention to songs that seem to be sending you a specific message. Consider the coincidence of information coming to you during these 9 days. And, be prepared to be more spontaneous and accept invitations. Offers that are presented during this time will have special significance.

Items for the 9 Day Energy Reset:

3 1-gallon jugs of distilled water

1 black permanent marking pen

Candle and wooden matches

1 index card

9 cups of Epsom salt, sea salt, or kosher salt

Pink Himalayan salt (optional if a health issue)

Obtain the above items at least 1 day before you begin this ritual. When you get these items home, set up a spot on your kitchen counter for the 3 bottles of distilled water. Create your energy-powered water. About 1 inch up from the bottom of each of the jugs of water, write the word "LOVE" with the permanent marker. Write this word on all 4 sides of all the jugs of water.

Set the 3 jugs in a row, with the first jug directly in front of you and the others lined up behind. Open the first jug in the row and add a pinch of the pink Himalayan salt. Replace the cap on the first jug (adding the salt is optional if there is a health issue).

At least twice daily, you will drink a glass of water; 1 each morning and 1 each night from the first jug until you finish it. After finishing the first jug of water, you will open the second jug, add a pinch of pink

Himalayan salt, and drink your twice daily water from that jug. You may or may not finish all 3 jugs over the 9 day period depending on how much and how often you are drinking the water. If you need to buy additional jugs, (because you choose to drink your energy water throughout the entire day), just add the word, "Love" to the bottom of the additional jug(s), and set it at the end of your water row.

Even if you do nothing else but drink this energy-powered water, you will notice change.

Suggested tasks during the 9 Day Energy Reset Ritual:

Write down 4 Personal Power Words that resonate with you about shifting your energy. If you cannot think of 4 words, you may choose any 4 words from the list below:

Love	Vibrant	Purpose
Health	Success	Prosperity
Kindness	Creative	Grateful
Awesome	Authentic	Spirit
Adventure	Brilliant	Energized
Connected	Spontaneous	Open

• Shortly after waking each day, drink one 8-12 oz. glass of water from the first "Love" jug

• Write down a goal that you would like to have happen on the index card. Tuck this card under your first jug of water. When you finish the first jug, place it under the next jug.

• Light the candle and say, "Thank you for the blessings and opportunities of my lifetime, now and ahead." Extinguish the candle.

• Exercise for 20 to 30 minutes (more is fine) — something with a regular tempo, such as: walking, biking, swimming, oscillating machine, or stair-stepper

• During the exercise, you will repeat your 4 Personal Power Words in your mind, in rhythm to the movement of your body. For example, simultaneously with your heel striking the ground as you walk, you will say one of the words, preceded by the words, "I am."

Heel strike = "I am Love"

Heel strike = "I am Health"

Heel strike = "I am Success"

Heel strike = "I am Prosperity"

Repeat for the entire length of the time you are exercising. When thoughts flow through your mind that may challenge your power words, let the next word act as a broom that sweeps the thought aside. If a brilliant idea comes to mind, add a word that represents that idea to your walking meditation. Write down your idea when you've finished your exercise.

• While showering/bathing after your exercise, imagine that any negative or limiting thoughts are being washed away from you.

• Get ready for your day. If it is a work day, embrace the thought that everyone at work is there to help you, even if it appears otherwise.

• The words you speak out loud are supportive, gentle and kind. And, as your Mom might have said, "If you can't say anything nice, don't say anything at all." You are not to verbally complain about anything to anyone. When someone asks how you are, respond with these words: "I have nothing to complain about." Be more interested in the other person than yourself. Notice if that person goes into "complaining" mode. If so, step back from that person for these 9 days.

• Stop yourself if you are tempted to allow negative words to spill out. Instead write the complaint, or unkind words, or just random mean thoughts, on the sticky side of a sticky note sheet. Then once you have written the words, seal the words by folding the sheet. Then, on the outside of this little envelope, write the words, "I release." Save the little envelope for when you get home.

• Keep a sticky note pad with you and when *anything* happens that upsets you, write about the incident on the sticky side of a sheet. Fold the paper to create a little envelope and write, "I release" on the outside of the note. Save the little envelope for when you get home.

• Eat so your body feels energized. When possible, avoid processed foods and sugar. Some people avoid any starchy, low energy foods during these 9 days, as well. As you eat, acknowledge the energy of the food as a gift to your body. The more natural the foods you consume, the better.

• Continue to take any medications as prescribed by your physician

• Take a high quality, daily vitamin

• If you like, you may drink your energy-powered water during the day. If you are a business owner, and serve water during your meetings, serving the energy-powered water will help to create a more productive gathering and meaningful dialogs.

• Give every person you interact with today a little extra attention. Imagine that the space between your eyebrows is relaxed and opening to receive information, inspiration, and love.

• If you do not work at a job, plan to be out of the house for at least a few hours per day. Even if it is to run errands, go to the library or a movie, browse at the store, or to visit with a friend.

• Accept all invitations. If folks at work all want to get together for a bowling night, or discount movie night, include yourself in the group activity.

• Make new friends by volunteering for something: dog or cat rescue, the library, a conservation group, a political gathering, or assisting at a children or senior home.

• When you get home for the day, safely burn any sticky note envelopes you have gathered.

• A few hours prior to bed, indulge in music, movies, or books that inspire or entertain you. Avoid newscasts, the Internet, and talk radio.

• Use evening or any free time to write, learn, or create. Write letters to people in your life that matter, and let them know you're thinking about them. Send a funny card to a friend, or send that long overdue thank you note.

• Avoid anything or anyone that has any potential to bring you pain. Avoid any activity that might make you feel sick or embarrassed. Take a vacation from any unhealthy habits – you know what they are. When you pay no attention to what is working *against* you, you will be able to recognize what will work *for* you.

• Avoid people who have treated you unkindly in any fashion.

• Avoid people who frequently ask you for something, or expect you to listen to their woes. If they call, let their phone call go to voice mail.

• Follow up, or explore, those brilliant ideas or creative projects of yours that might lead you in a new direction.

• Bake cookies, or a treat for delivery to someone, on one of the days of your 9 day reset. Maybe for that mechanic who fixed a flat tire for you some months ago, or didn't charge you for that something extra. Deliver cookies to the employees of the restaurant you like to visit. Or, if you don't want to cook, but still want to express your gratitude, a few dozen donuts work just as well. The more random the kindness, the more powerful it is.

• Each of these 9 days, insert a $1.00 bill into a stamped envelope and address it to a local charity. You can send more if you like, but do not write your address on the return section of the envelope. Instead, draw a picture of a heart in that space. You will mail this tomorrow as the first task of the day when you leave the house. Maybe donate $1.00 per day to that collection box, when you check out at the grocery store. Make it a priority to give away a dollar a day.

• About 30 minutes before bedtime, take a bath with 1 cup of the Epsom, sea, or kosher salt. While in the bathtub, imagine that any negativity is being pulled out of your body by the salt. Think about what you almost said to someone that was unkind, or a complaint. Congratulate yourself for your restraint. Relax into the idea that you are being guided to your ideal energy, and bless yourself for staying true to your intent. Relax in your bath for at least 5 minutes. When you release the water from the tub, stand and imagine that any remaining negativity is being pulled from the bottom of your feet, and flowing down the drain. If you do not have a bathtub, or it is difficult for you to get into one, fill a foot-soaking tub with warm water and dissolve 1 cup of Epsom salt. Soak your feet for 5 to 10 minutes and imagine that all the negativity is being pulled from you through your feet by the salt. When you empty the water from the foot tub down the drain, imagine that the negativity is flowing far away from you.

• A few minutes before bed, drink a glass of water from your jug of "Love" water.

• Light the candle and speak aloud, "Thank you for the blessings and opportunities of this day, and the ones coming into my life." Feel in your heart true gratitude and thank anyone and everyone that was pleasant to you today, even if it was the clerk at the store. Extinguish the candle.

• When you get into bed, inhale deeply (counting to 6 as you inhale) saying the word, "Love" and then release (for the count of 6) the word, "Fear." Inhale in the essence of "Love," and exhale out "Fear" 3 times. Then, (count of 6 again), inhale the essence of "Love," and exhale the essence of "Love" 3 times. Then concentrate on the words, "I am love" and allow yourself to sleep.

Even if you only drink a glass of this energy-powered water each morning upon waking, and another each evening before bed, you will notice a difference.

However, if you really want to see and experience a major difference, follow at least half of the tasks/perspectives/attitudes above and drink your energy-powered water throughout your day. Even doing a few of the added tasks each day will enhance this ritual. You may do some of them on one day, and others on another.

As your energy becomes lighter and more accepting, you may notice that people will attempt to ask more of you. You may notice that people that you have not heard from for some time will contact you. It's about you receiving the message of that contact, not an immediate obligation for you to act. Some of these people have categorized you into a specific identity. They assume that by making a call to you that you will respond for their benefit in some way. Listen and absorb the messages from people, but do not, unless it benefits you, allow yourself to be talked into a contribution or action.

The exception to this is to anyone that you owe a favor or good turn. Someone has done something that benefitted you in the past, and that person is asking for your help. That is the person to whom you should extend your good will. We are all here in this world to assist each other with our lessons, and with our path. It feels good to give back, and it feels especially good when you can be there for someone that was there for you.

For these 9 days you will place the majority of your energy in receiving, not giving. Expect an offer or a breakthrough in understanding during these 9 days. Any action you take during this 9 Day Energy Reset will only better you in some way.

Remember to utilize the ways to decline any assumptive invitations or requests, which are found in the "You ARE Love" section of this guide.

You will know when this is working when you seem lighter and more at peace. You'll begin to see people react to you with a kinder and more helpful demeanor. Even if you adopt just a few of the above suggestions, they will allow you to experience a more meaningful shift.

Be watchful, aware, and accept anything that comes to you. You may become inspired to write a book, or you may meet someone who offers you a job or a fun experience. Expect that new things will be attracted to you from unexpected places. Listen to the words people tell you as though they are specifically intended for your ears. Be attentive of things happening that give you ideas to align with a new future for you. Agree that the world is actually working for you and your best interests.

If you are a small business owner, you will notice that you will begin to receive more interest in your service or product. You are operating on a higher frequency than before. New ideas may come to you because you are open to receiving more, rather than giving more. Be grateful and accept. When you find yourself idle, do the groundwork and preparation for your own success. You are changing your energy to change your life.

Even if something doesn't go the way you expect, be grateful for everything. You are love, and you are being guided by love. If something cancels, have something else meaningful to do to distract you. Avoid dwelling in what you think is going wrong, and instead concentrate on the things that you are doing to be better. Direct your thinking to be in the mindset of living in and planning for your success.

You may repeat (or continue) this ritual upon completion. Most have found that when they live in this energy of love and receptivity, little and big miracles appear. When they release the expectation that things have to happen a certain way, and are instead open for things to happen a better way, that is exactly what happens.

All is exactly as it should be because you are being guided by the Power of Love.

Made in the USA
San Bernardino, CA
28 December 2018